THE
PLEASURES
OF

PLAYING
GOLF

ABERCROMBIE & FITCH

LIBRARY

BOOKSELLERS
EST. 1892

An Ode to Golf

We give the complete text of the most quoted poem on golf. We believe it was published in America during the war, but we have been unable to trace the author. Can any of our readers help us?

A SCIENTIST

They do not know what Golf may be
  Who call it childish play,
To drive a globule from a tee
  And follow it away.
They do not understand who scoff
  And all its virtues miss,
Who think that this is all of Golf,
  For Golf is more than this.

For Golf is earth's ambassador
  That comes to haunts of men,
To lure them from the banking floor,
  The counter and the pen.
To lead them gently by the hand
  From toil and stress and strife,
And guide them through the summer
  Along the path of life.

The pastime of philosophers,
  For such a man must be,
When far away the golf ball whirrs

A POLITICIAN

2

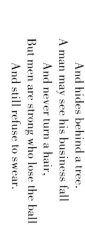

A FILM-STAR

And hides behind a tree.
A man may see his business fall
And never turn a hair,
But men are strong who lose the ball
And still refuse to swear.

It is a game of honour, too,
That tries the souls of men:
It's easy in the public view
To be all honest then.
But he deserves an angel's wings
Who paths of truth has trod,
When left alone with just two things —
His score card and his God.

If Golf shall teach you patiently
Adversity to meet;
If it shall teach philosophy
To keep your temper sweet;
If it shall teach you still to grin
With mirth no matter what,
You are a victor if you win
A loving cup or not.

Anon, *poem from World War 1*

A GENERAL

"And Thou Shalt Woo Her . . ."

Golf is a fickle game, and must be wooed to be won. No good can be got by forcing the game; and unless one feels fit and has a keen interest in the match, it is better not to play. It is no use going out and playing around in a half-hearted, listless, indifferent way. Playing in this way is ruinous to good golf. . . .

Further, golf is a business-like game, and should be gone about in a brisk, business-like way. It is far better to play and walk round the links smartly and quickly than to creep round at a snail-like pace. It is impossible to play good golf if you are thinking of something else all the time, and if you have any business worries, leave them behind when you go on the links.

William Park Junior

The SPUR

PUBLISHED BY

THE ANGUS COMPANY

J.A. McKAY, President

389 FIFTH AVENUE, NEW YORK

60 RUE CAUMARTIN
PARIS

9 CHARING CROSS ROAD
LONDON

WHEN YOUR DRIVE IS GOING FINE

When your drive is going fine,
  – 250 every shot –
Then you're sure to dub the putts.
  (At least as sure as not.)
When you pitch your "mashies" up
  And drop them near the hole,
You still have trouble with the putts
  And find they will not roll.
Then one day you start to play;
  You tee up with a grin.
"As long as I can keep my drive
  'Twill be a cinch to win."
To your surprise you top it first,
  And then you hit the tee.
The reason for your change in form,
  You cannot clearly see.
Instead you find the putts will sink;
  You cannot seem to fail.
You drop them from the farthest edge,
  And your opponents quail.
Another day your mashie work
  Is far below the par.
But then you play your niblick shots
  Like some high-rated star.
You cannot seem to play one round
  With each shot going good.
– But then, you'd soon put Braid and
  Vardon
Out of business if you could.

Golfers Magazine, 1915

THE EVENING ROUND

There is, of course, one ideal method of playing golf on a summer's day, if only the players have time enough, and that is by one morning and one evening round and a long and blissful snooze between lunch and tea. How often have we felt and said, as we start home weary after the day's golf, "Now would be the time to start". There is nothing so heavenly as an evening round when the heat of the day has abated and part of the course is in shadow. Yet we only play that round, as a rule, when it is the only one possible after a day's work in an office. On a holiday we have not always enough self-control to wait for that divine coolness. We pound away in the sun, and when the time comes we are prostrate.

Bernard Darwin

THAT DAMNED SCOTCH CROQUET

Two Englishmen, it is said, visited St Andrews in the course of a Scotch tour. Looking out of a window of the train at the point where the railway runs along the links, they took their first survey of the game. The weather had been very wet, and at the bottom of some bunkers water was lying. "These are the places," said A to B with ready ingenuity, "where the Scotch play curling in winter." "No," said B to A, "these are the holes they use for golf, and the object of the player is to get out of one into another as quickly as he can manage it." Armed with this superior knowledge, A proceeds down to the links, and finds an old gentleman struggling with destiny at the bottom of a bad bunker. At last the player succeeds in getting out his ball, but only with the result of sending it into the next bunker a few yards farther on. This is not an agreeable incident under any circumstances at golf; but conceive, if you can, the irritation of the player when he finds himself being loudly and, as he no doubt thinks, ironically congratulated by a spectator on the results of his stroke and the well-merited success with which it has been rewarded!

I do not know whether this story is apocryphal or not, but in any case the ignorance which it displays is not likely to be long continued in the southern portions of the island. There will soon be more greens in England than in Scotland, and more players of English extraction than of Scotch. "Do you have much play here?" said someone to the keeper of a racket-court in the neighbourhood of an English golf links. "We used to, sir," said the man, "but ever since this d——d Scotch croquet has come into fashion, no one comes into the court!"

On the Green, Lord Balfour, 1922

Westward Ho!

In 1882 I left Oxford, with the intention of reading for the Bar, and actually did go so far as to eat a number of Inner Temple dinners at the extraordinary hour of six o'clock. I do not think they are quite digested yet. I had been suffering from a series of severe headaches all through my last year at Oxford, and perhaps the dinners put a finishing touch on them. At all events, the doctors advised me to give up all reading for a time, an instruction which I have observed rather faithfully up to the present. Their very wise counsel gave me all the more time for golf – the rules were not quite so many and headachy then, and a man could play golf, or so it seems to me, with a lighter heart. Perhaps it is only because the heart had less weight of years to carry then, but it strikes me that the game and its players had more humour. I do not mean that they were more witty; but greatly because they were so immensely serious and solemn and earnest they were more amusing. Their tempers were more tempestuous, their language was infinitely more picturesque.

On the Green, Horace G. Hutchinson, 1922

THE HEIRLOOM

The Championship Belt was played for in the early days. Willie Park won it on three different occasions, and I won it on four, but not year after year. Then my son Tommy was the winner of it for three years running (1868, 1869 and 1870), and it became his own property for good. I have the belt in my house now, and it is the proudest possession that I have – in my eyes it is absolutely priceless. It is composed of a big, broad belt of dark red morocco leather, with rich golfing designs in silver upon it as ornaments.

I could also show you two photographs – extremely interesting and valuable to me – of my two sons, Tommy and Jimmy. They are in one frame, and underneath the pictures are printed their best scores round St. Andrews links, and curiously enough the totals are exactly the same – 77. Tommy did it in 1869, going out in 37 strokes and returning in 40, and in 1887 Jimmy went out in 38 and came home in 39, both 77.

"Old Tom" Morris

CHURCHMAN'S CIGARETTES.

TOM MORRIS.

WORTHY COMBAT

Golf is the peculiar game of a peculiar people; its trend is onward on parallel lines; it is the pastime of the Scots.

John L. Low

Golf may be played on Sunday, not being a game within the view of the law, but being a form of moral effort.

John L. Low

Golf is not a wrestle with Bogey; it is not a struggle with your mortal foe; it is a physiological, psychological, and moral fight with yourself; it is a test of mastery over self; and the ultimate and irreducible element of the game is to determine which of the players is the more worthy combatant.

John L. Low

A Caddie
Who Couldn't Speak English

A young player, wintering at Pau, in France, and almost wholly ignorant of the language, had for his caddie a French boy who knew no English. They managed to get on by the language of signs. At last the player made a remarkably good approach shot, and his ball lying dead, he turned round with an air of intense satisfaction and triumph to his caddie, who instantly exclaimed, "Beastly fluke!" It was all the English that he knew.

On the Green, Findlay S. Douglas, 1922

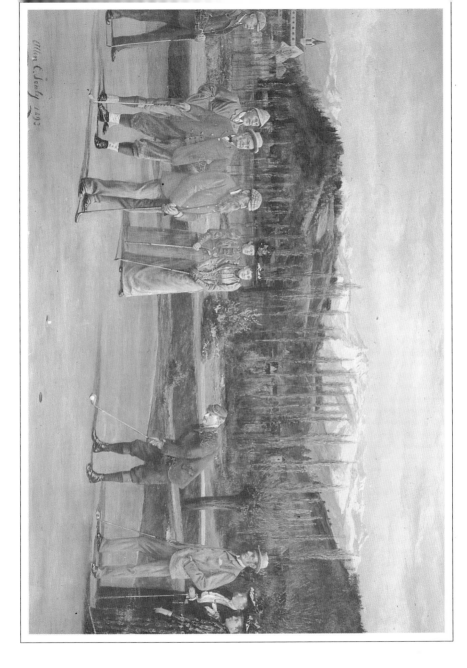

PUTTERS ARE FEMININE

About the putter there is something so slender and sensitive, so fitful, capricious and fickle, shall I venture to say even at times inconstant, that no doubt can be felt as to the sex question. Plainly, such a companion will not readily be chanced on among the common herd or met with in the crowded street: she must be sought for with care and skill. No club is so human as the putter, none so worthy the name of friend, if true, no more likely to do one an injury if disloyal and treacherous. Like so many of her sex, the putter has a touch of vanity in her nature which must be humoured, if she is to be won as a faithful mistress.

John L. Low

THE MASTER STROKE

Which is the master stroke in golf? I say that it is the ball struck by any club to which a big pull or slice is intentionally applied for the accomplishment of a specific purpose which could not be achieved in any other way. . . . I call it the master shot because, to accomplish it with any certainty and perfection, it is so difficult even to the experienced golfer; because it calls for the most absolute command over the club and every nerve and sinew of the body, and because, when properly done, it is a splendid thing to see, and for a certainty results in material gain to the man who played it.

Harry Vardon

ROBERT TYRE JONES

Mr Jones is the supreme modern instance of having so regulated his game that he gives the fewest hostages to fortune. His opponents find it difficult to play against him not merely because of his reputation and the consistency of his scoring but because he has a temperament which nothing seems to affect. He is heartbreaking in his astonishing freedom from error. Most players have a breaking-point; to all appearances Mr Jones has none. He is inflexible, and the other man has no option except to bend.

The Perfect Golfer, H.N. Wethered, 1931

R. T. JONES

THE UNIVERSAL GAME

Golf is the only game where the worst player gets the best of it. He obtains more out of it as regards both exercise and enjoyment, for the good player gets worried over the slightest mistake, whereas the poor player makes too many mistakes to worry over them.

David Lloyd George

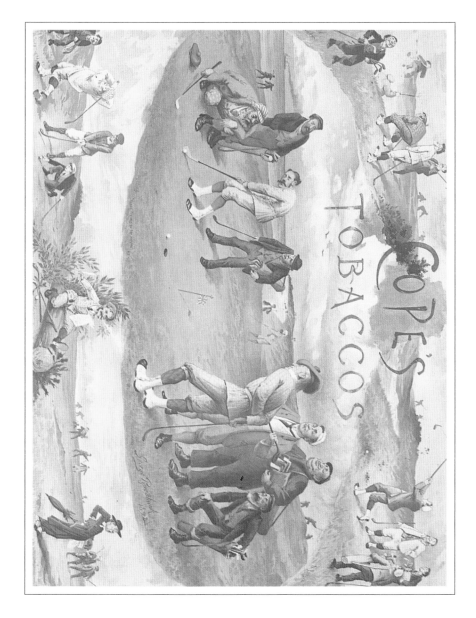

AN AMERICAN LOOKS AT ST ANDREWS

St Andrews is really and truly the golfer's paradise. Everybody in that town of some six thousand residents is interested in the game. Male and female, children and elderly people, all play golf in some form or other. There is an hotel called "Golf Hotel", but for that matter all hotels or boarding-houses harbour golfers. There are golf shops everywhere, where one can buy anything from a club or ball to a golf suit or a fancy-coloured golf umbrella.

In 1923 the American boys had reservations at the Grand Hotel, which was less than a fair-sized approach putt from the eighteenth green. In late May or early June the twilight of the long Scottish evenings carries on to eleven o'clock. It was nothing at all unusual to see four-ball matches coming up the eighteenth fairway as late as ten-thirty, and since American golfers were in the habit of retiring at that hour, after thirty-six holes of golf, they were often soothed to sleep by the click of club-heads meeting balls.

The wonderful club, known as the Royal and Ancient, should not be forgotten, because it adds to the dignity of the place. This, of course, is where the rules of golf were laid down, and every development of the clubs and balls has its own cabinet for displaying the implements that have given to the world at large so much pleasure. Magnificent trophies, too, are sights well worth the golfers' interest. A simple stone building, one can recline in the easy-chairs and think nothing but the most pleasant things. It is the atmosphere that is so thrilling – golf, and nothing but golf.

A Game of Golf, Francis Ouimet

Quitting Business to Play Golf

O ld Colonel Bogey invaded the roar and bustle of the La Salle Street station recently and sent in his card to H.U. Mudge, president of the Chicago, Rock Island & Pacific Railway, and joint receiver of the property.

Mr Mudge fussed impatiently about the papers on his desk, and looked out of the window with an eye that did not see the elevated railroad nor the all-circling smoke. Thus does the summons of golf and Colonel Bogey affect those who have the fever.

"Forty-three years have I been railroading," mused Mr Mudge. "Now I want to play golf a little.

"Golf isn't a game; it's a philosophy. It is a substitute for the philosophy of business, and as essential. Only recently have men come to know that. Therefore we shall be better men henceforth.

"It is not only a philosophy; it is an elixir of youth and vim.

"It is not only an elixir of youth, but a sweetener of dispositions; therefore, it is a tonic for souls.

"And, therefore, I hope Judge Carpenter will accept my resignation as receiver at once and let me play the game."

Golfers Magazine, November 1915

DON'T TAKE GOLF TOO SERIOUSLY

Don't take your golf too seriously is the advice given in an eastern exchange by a well-known golfer who has figured in tournament play for several years and who admits now to having wasted the early years of his golfing career because he took his games as a matter of life and death.

"I never commenced to really enjoy the game," said he, "until I found out it was only a pastime instead of a business. At first I was so keen on winning that I could not rest at night when I was to play a match the next day. Every little old cup that I played for seemed to be the most important thing in the world at that time. If I failed to win my family had to suffer, as I became a regular grouch around the house."

Golfers Magazine, November 1915

AFTER GOLF—

A
MUSTARD
BATH

THE CURLED NIBLICK FOR GETTING ROUND THINGS

A NEAT DRIVER (for beginners) WITH OBVIOUS ADVANTAGES

THE FEATHER-HEADED NIBLICK FOR TICKLISH WORK

THE WATER-PROOF MASHIE FOR KEEPING THE CLOTHES DRY ON DAMP COURSES

THE LIFTING IRON FOR GETTING BALLS OUT OF IMPOSSIBLE POSITIONS

THE TELESCOPIC PUTTER TO SAVE THE LEGS

W. HEATH ROBINSON

THE NEW PUTTER FITTED WITH PATENT BALL GUIDER

THE GOLFER'S SUCTION PUMP FOR DISCOVERING LOST BALLS

A MOVABLE BUNKER

THE GOLFER'S SAFETY HAT

AN OBSTACLE REMOVER

W. HEATH ROBINSON

"N.B."

He's not very handsome or classy,
He's not very dressy or bright,
He shoots round a hundred and twenty
With form absolutely a fright.
He's rather inclined to bad language,
To style he was never a serf,
But there's one thing for which he is blessed –
He always replaces the turf.

Locker Room Ballads, W. Hastings Webling, 1925

AN AFFECTATION OF NOMENCLATURE

The very names of the clubs were alluring. As I recall them, the usual set included the driver or "play-club" – an affectation of nomenclature from the old Scotch school – invariably shod with a strip of something that looked like horn; the brassie; the cleek (a popular club then) and some irons and a putter.

The Autobiography of an Average Golfer, O.B. Keeler, 1925

THE MASTER EYE IN GOLF

Very few golfers are aware there is such a thing as a master eye. About 75 per cent of human beings have the right as master eye, which is as it should be if the player turns his head only slightly. If he turns more, his master eye vision is obscured by the bridge of his nose, and the difference between the view he had in the address and the view at the top of the back swing is about two inches, quite sufficient to lead to chronic inaccuracy.

Golfers Magazine, November 1915

The Golfer's Alphabet

"American Golfer" – liked by all
Brassie, Bunker and Ball
Caddy, Club-house and Club
Divot – also for "Dub"
Energy that we get from Nature's store
Foozle, Foursome and Fore
Golf – the Greatest of Games
Hazards and Holes – some with odd names
Iron – and In – the last nine
Joy – from the "Game Divine"
Kick – of both player and ball
Links – enjoyed Spring, Summer and Fall
Mashie, Marker and "Muck"
Niblick – sometimes used with great luck
Out – the first nine – just half through
Putter – and Putting which must be made true
Quiet; must be observed during play
Rub of the Green, very careless they say
Stymie, Slice, Score and Skill
Tee, and Top when the ball you try to kill
Useful, and means a good shot
Vim and Vigor, you develop a lot
Win, which gives you great delight
"Xcuse," when a shot is not right
Young – the game keeps one youthful
Zeal – which makes one be truthful

Golfers Magazine, January 1913

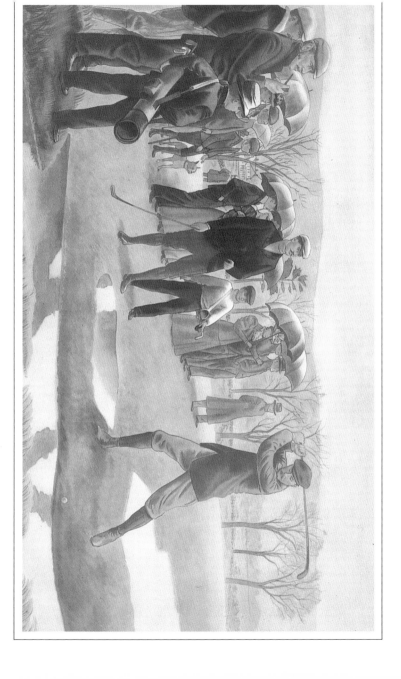

HINTS ON GOLF

Of any player of any game it is almost always high praise to say that he plays freely, and this laudable attribute of freedom makes, I think, no bad text for a golfing discourse. It can be of the right kind and it can also be of a very decidedly wrong kind, through the cultivation of which the player becomes a slave to various bad habits for the rest of his golfing life.

When the bad golfer watches the good golfer, he sees many things that make him jealous, and that which he envies perhaps most bitterly of all is the litheness, the dash, the "young, insolent fearlessness," as it has been well called, of the full swing. The way in which every ounce of weight and muscle is put into the blow, while the club and the body of the player seem to be flung simultaneously at the ball, is certainly one of the jolliest – if one may so call it – one of the most inspiring spectacles that any game has to offer. It is also for him who would emulate what he sees, one of the most teasing and deceitful.

Hints on Golf by Bernard Darwin for Burberry's, 1912

FOR HE'S A GOLFER

To win the cup and championship,
He may not have the skill,
But he will always do his best
With self-control and will.
That he's a thorough gentleman
Is more important still,
For he's a golfer.

He never tries to jar you
At your putts and little chips.
He wins his matches with his clubs
And never with his lips.
Or loses with a cheerful smile
That nothing can eclipse,
For he's a golfer.

So greet him when you meet him
While playing through the green
Salute him with your waving hand,
And most respectful mein,
And catch an inspiration,
From his countenance serene,
To be a golfer.

Golfers Magazine, November 1915

To My VALENTINE

Though a Golfing Match is most famous sport,
A much better match it would be
With hands united and true hearts plighted.
A Love Match to make with me.

WILLING TO LEARN.

WAGGLERS

Most women golfers are elaborate wagglers, but none that Bradbury had ever seen had made quite such a set of Swedish exercises out of the simple act of laying the club-head behind the ball and raising it over the right shoulder. For fully a minute, it seemed to him, Mrs Fisher fiddled and pawed at the ball; while Bradbury, realizing that there are eighteen tees on a course and that this Russian Ballet stuff was consequently going to happen at least seventeen times more, quivered in agony and clenched his hands till the knuckles stood out white under the strain. Then she drove, and the ball trickled down the hill into a patch of rough some five yards distant.

'Tee-hee!' said Mrs Fisher.

Bradbury uttered a sharp cry. He was married to a golfing giggler!

The Heart of a Goof, P.G. Wodehouse, 1926

GOLFING KIT

L ove of comfort and luxury has recently produced a supine indifference to ceremonial attitudes. This has tended to establish as a custom the practice of wearing a *dégagé* and rustic garb under circumstances formerly requiring with peremptory insistence – only flouted by the very rich, rude, or eccentric – a habit of austere hue and funereal severity of cut. Many have availed themselves of this licence, but none so eagerly as the golfer.

Hints on Golf by Bernard Darwin for Burberry's, 1912

We own that at first sight it is difficult for the uninitiated looker-on to sympathise with the evident enthusiasm of the players. There does not seem to be anything very stimulating in grinding round a barren stretch of ground, impelling a gutta-percha ball before you, striving to land it in a succession of small holes in fewer strokes than your companion and opponent. But as to the reality of the excitement, you are soon compelled to take that for granted. You see gentlemen of all ages, often of the most self-indulgent or sedentary habits, turning out in every kind of weather, persevering to the dusk of a winter day, in spite of bitter wind and driving showers; or dragging about their cumbrous weight of flesh in hot defiance of the most sultry summer temperature. The truth is that, appearances notwithstanding, experience proves it to be one of the most fascinating of pursuits; nor can there be any question that it is among the most invigorating. You play it on some stretch of ground by the sea, generally sheltered more or less by rows of hummocky sandhills which break the force of the breeze without intercepting its freshness. You keep moving for the most part, although there is no need for moving faster than is necessary to set the blood in healthy circulation. In a tournament like that which ended on Wednesday at St Andrews, you select your own partner. The deep-chested, strapping young fellows in their prime, with the reach of arm and strength of shoulder that make their swing so tremendous in driving the ball, pair off together. The obese and elderly gentlemen, touched in the wind by time, and doubtful subjects for insurance offices, may jog along placidly at their own pace.

There is exhilaration in the brisk walk round the links in the fresh sea air, but it is the culminating excitement of the critical moments on the putting greens which gives the national game its universal zest. *Once a golfer you are always a golfer.*

The Times, 5 October 1874

A Cow Story

President Dan McDonald, of the Lakeside Country Club, Tacoma, has a new cow story. He tells of playing the first hole at Lakeside. His drive was a good one. The mashie pitch went wild and struck a friendly cow that had invaded the golf course. With a dead "thump" it struck her side. Resenting the blow, she kicked just as the ball fell to the ground. The result was a nice pitch to the green which was holed out in one putt. Justice De Witt M. Evans was a witness of the incident.

Golfers Magazine, December 1915

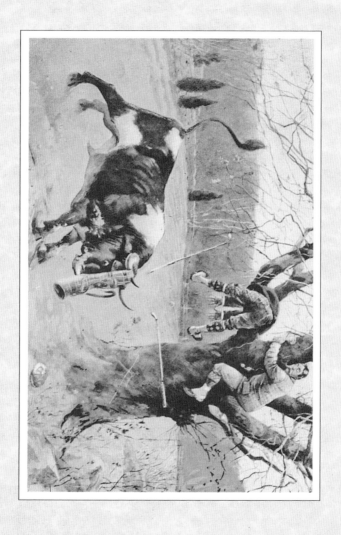

Golf Dreams

No close observer of the golfer has recorded whether any phenomena are to be observed in him during sleep; whether, like a dreaming greyhound, his limbs move in conformity with the occupations of the day. It is ascertained beyond question that he dreams about golf: dreams how he hit a ball which seemed as if it would never come down, and, when it did, fell into the next hole a quarter of a mile away; dreams how he habitually holes out at thirty yards, and how neither "bunkers" nor whins can hold him. All this, and much more, he has been known to dream; but as yet no complaints have been lodged by indignant wives of blows received during the watches of the night from hands wielding imaginary golf clubs; so we must assume that he reclines peacefully, especially as, if there existed cause of complaint on this score, we should hear of it from those ladies who are unsympathetic to the game.

Anon

A GOLFER'S NIGHTMARE.

ACKNOWLEDGEMENTS

PICTURE CREDITS

Unless otherwise indicated, all illustrations are from the collection of Sarah Fabian Baddiel, Golfiana, Grays In The Mews, London W1Y 1AR 071 408 1239.

Front cover: *Westward Ho!* Michael Brown (Hon Osmond Scott, Hon Denys Scott, Capt. Molesworth RN, Horace Hutchinson, Capt Prideux Brune).

Title page: *Unpublished Study of Golfers for Kipling's Almanack of Twelve Sports* (Bridgeman/Private Collection)

2-3 *The Finishes of the Famous*, Frank Reynolds
5 *Cover of "The Spur"*, 1914
7 *The Putt* Anon (The Golf Collection)
9 *Presuick, Himalaya Hole*, Michael Brown (G. Duncan, J. H. Taylor, James Braid, Harry Vardon)
11 *John Whyte Melville*, Sir Francis Grant (Bridgeman Art Library/Royal & Ancient Golf Club, St. Andrews)
13 *Golfing at Westward Ho!* Francis Powell Hopkins (Bridgeman/Private Collection)
15 *Tom Morris at a Refreshment Barrow on the Links* (St. Andrews University Library, Cowie Collection)
17 *Driving Off, 1894*, Peter Adamson (Royal & Ancient Golf Club, St. Andrews)
19 *Golfers at Pau, 1892*, Allen C. Sealy
21 *Aberdony Ladies Championship, 1901*, Michael Brown
23 *The Great Triumvirate, 1913*, Clement Flower (Bridgeman/Private Collection)
25 *R. T. Jones* (Hulton Picture Company)
27 *Cope's Tobacco*
29 *Hole O'Cross, St. Andrews 1892* (The Golf Collection)

31 *Cover of Golfers Magazine, 1915*
33 *The Humours of Golf*, W. Heath Robinson
34 *Hatching the Ball*, W. Heath Robinson
35 *Unfortunate Golfer*, Lawson Wood, c. 1920's
37 *Men Wearing Norfolk Jackets*. Taken from travellers samples for the cloth manufacturers USA c. 1915.
39 *Golfers at Holy Island. Links. Northumberland*. An early railway publicity photograph from the London. North Eastern Railway Co. c.1900
41 *The First Amateur Golf Championships, USA. 1895*, after Everett Henry (United States Golfing Association)
43 *Coming Home, St. Andrews*, Michael Brown
45 *Valentine cards c.1910-20*
47 *Golfing at Monte Carlo* (Hulton Picture Company)
49 *The Prince of Wales, later King Edward VIII*. Sir William Orpen (Royal & Ancient Golf Club, St. Andrews)
51 *Westward Ho!* Michael Brown
53 *Up the Tree . . . .*
55 *The Funny Side of Golf: The Golfers Nightmare*

TEXT CREDITS

Text extracts from the following sources are reprinted with the kind permission of the publishers and copyright holders stated. Should any copyright holder have been inadvertently omitted they should apply to the publishers who will be pleased to credit them in any subsequent editions.

8, 42, 48: Bernard Darwin (courtesy of Duckworths)
46 P. G. Wodehouse, *The Heart of A Goof* (A. P. Watt Ltd on behalf of the Trustees of the Wodehouse Estate; Barrie & Jenkins Ltd. Random Century)

First published in Great Britain 1991 for
ABERCROMBIE & FITCH, INC.
by Pavilion Books Limited
196 Shaftesbury Avenue, London WC2H 8JL.

Anthology compilation copyright © Jenny de Gex 1991
From the collection of Sarah Fabian Baddiel, Golfiana,
Gray's In The Mews, London W1
For other copyright holders see Acknowledgements.

Designed by Andrew Barron & Collis Clements Associates

A CIP catalogue record for this book is available
from the British Library

ISBN 1-85145-784-4

Printed and bound in Scotland by Eagle Colour Books